JOSSEY-BASS TEACHER

Jossey-Bass Teacher provides educators with practical knowledge and tools to create a positive and lifelong impact on student learning. We offer classroom-tested and research-based teaching resources for a variety of grade levels and subject areas. Whether you are an aspiring, new, or veteran teacher, we want to help you make every teaching day your best.

From ready-to-use classroom activities to the latest teaching framework, our value-packed books provide insightful, practical, and comprehensive materials on the topics that matter most to K–12 teachers. We hope to become your trusted source for the best ideas from the most experienced and respected experts in the field.

D0204102

i

HOW TO TEACH ENGLISH LANGUAGE LEARNERS

Effective Strategies from Outstanding Educators

DIANE HAAGER

JANETTE K. KLINGNER

TERESE C. ACEVES

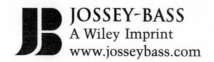
JOSSEY-BASS
A Wiley Imprint
www.josseybass.com

Published by Jossey-Bass
A Wiley Imprint
989 Market Street, San Francisco, CA 94103-1741—www.josseybass.com

Jossey-Bass books and products are available through most bookstores. To contact Jossey-Bass directly call our Customer Care Department within the U.S. at 800-956-7739, outside the U.S. at 317-572-3986, or fax 317-572-4002.

Jossey-Bass also publishes its books in a variety of electronic formats. Some content that appears in print may not be available in electronic books.

Library of Congress Cataloging-in-Publication Data

Haager, Diane.
  How to teach English language learners : effective strategies from outstanding educators / Diane Haager, Janette K. Klingner, Terese C. Aceves.
       p. cm. – (Jossey-Bass teacher)
  Includes bibliographical references and index.
  ISBN 978-0-470-39005-4 (pbk.)
  1. English language–Study and teaching–foreign speakers. I. Klingner, Janette K. II. Aceves, Terese C., 1970- III. Title.
  PE1128.A2H223 2009
  428.2'4–dc22
                              2009031944
Printed in the United States of America

FIRST EDITION

PB Printing 10 9 8 7 6 5 4 3 2 1

ABOUT THIS BOOK

We often learn the most by watching those who are highly skilled perform their craft and then trying the new ideas ourselves. This book provides an opportunity to do just that by shining a light into the classrooms of successful elementary school teachers and their English language learners (ELLs) and depicting strategies for teaching reading and language arts while also supporting students' language acquisition. The book includes scenarios from bilingual and English immersion models in various schools and contexts where we will find ELLs. These case studies highlight instruction across three tiers of reading instruction typical of a Response to Intervention (RTI) model: core reading and language arts instruction, small-group supplemental reading intervention for struggling readers, and intensive instruction for students with learning disabilities. Each chapter includes opportunities for reflection through questions for the readers and suggested application activities. This book is for readers who want to learn how to improve outcomes for English language learners, and it is appropriate for group study, in professional learning communities or teacher education classes, or for individual reading.

THE AUTHORS

Diane Haager is a professor at California State University, Los Angeles, where she instructs teachers in methods for teaching students with reading difficulties and learning disabilities. Haager has worked in the public schools as a reading specialist and special educator. She is coauthor with Janette K. Klingner of *Differentiating Instruction in Inclusive Classrooms: The Special Educator's Guide* (Allyn & Bacon, 2004), and she coauthored the reading intervention handbook *Interventions for Reading Success* (Brookes, 2007), as well as numerous book chapters and articles. Haager's research interests include effective reading instruction for English learners, students with learning disabilities, and students at risk for reading failure.

Janette K. Klingner is a professor of education specializing in bilingual multicultural special education at the University of Colorado at Boulder. She was a bilingual special education teacher for ten years before earning a PhD in reading and learning disabilities from the University of Miami. To date, she has authored or coauthored more than eighty articles, books, and book chapters. In 2004 she won the American Educational Research Association's Early Career Award. Research interests include reading comprehension strategy instruction for culturally and linguistically diverse students, Response to Intervention for English language learners, the disproportionate representation of culturally and linguistically diverse students in special education, and professional development that enhances teacher quality.

Terese C. Aceves is an associate professor of special education at Loyola Marymount University in Los Angeles. After working in the classroom as a bilingual resource specialist, she earned her PhD in special education, disabilities, and risk studies from the University of California, Santa Barbara, while also completing her masters degree in school psychology. She is coeditor of *Education for All: Critical Issues in the Education of Children and Youth with Disabilities* (Jossey-Bass, 2008). Her research interests include early intervention and identification of children at risk for reading failure and supporting culturally and linguistically diverse families who have children with disabilities.

ACKNOWLEDGMENTS

We are teacher-educators and researchers with a constant thirst for learning how to improve outcomes for all children—particularly culturally and linguistically diverse students and students with special needs. Our inspiration for this book came from our desire to help teachers see effective instruction in action. Through our research, we have encountered amazing teachers who have been successful with English language learners. We wish to help others learn from their successful practices.

We are very grateful for the teachers who have allowed us to come into their classrooms and learn from what they do. Only a few of them are represented in this book. We are grateful to the principals and teachers who have welcomed us into their schools, permitted us to observe in their classrooms, and talked with us about what they do for their students. We hope there will always be such welcoming professionals who are willing to share their practices, so that all can benefit from their expertise.

All the teachers depicted in this book participated in school-based research projects. We are grateful for the research teams who helped us manage the projects, collect data, conduct interviews, and analyze our findings, including Michelle Windmueller, Joe Dimino, Jennifer Mahdavi, Danessa Murdock, Josefa Rascón, Beth Harry, Angela Deterville, and Keith Sturges.

We thank our wonderful editor, Marjorie McAneny, and the production team at Jossey-Bass, who have offered excellent suggestions, encouraged us, and supported our efforts. It has been a pleasure to work with each of you!

Lastly, we thank our families and friends, who have been patient and encouraging, always believing that our writing is important and will help the teachers who read it. Thanks to Steve Haager, Emily Haager, Julia Devin, Carmina Aceves, Raul Aceves, Ignacio Higareda, Irma Vazquez, Donald Klingner, Heidi Warden, John Klingner, and Amy Previato.

Diane Haager: To those who shaped my thinking about teaching as we taught together, especially Gail Wagner, Tom Wagner, Bea Raddant, Opal Hamm, Sue Stark, and Paul Heithaus. Also to the children I have taught, many of whom were learning English as a second language while learning to read and write. I have learned so much from you all!

Janette K. Klingner: To the many outstanding bilingual educators I had the privilege of working with and learning from during my years as a resource specialist at Anne Darling Elementary School in San Jose, California. Among them were bilingual teachers Beverly Basalla, Trini Warren, Juan Herrera, Adele Montenegro, and Sue Sartor; the counselor Jesse Aguirre; the paraprofessional who worked with me in our trilingual resource room, Elizabeth Sousa; and our principal, Cecilia Espalin-Huffman. Together we made a difference!

Terese C. Aceves: To the numerous teachers and administrators I had the opportunity and pleasure to work with and observe as a graduate student and beginning researcher. Also to my colleagues and friends within the Lennox School District and specifically at Jefferson Elementary School. During all my work in the schools I have never met a more dedicated group of teachers and administrators committed to supporting students with and without disabilities and their families.

CONTENTS